RELATIONSHIPS
GROUP BIBLE STUDY

WRITTEN BY

Karen Helsel, Jerry Hickson, Sharon Bernhardt, and Kevin Stiffler

Relationships: Group Bible Study

Written by Karen Helsel, Jerry Hickson, Sharon Bernhardt, and Kevin Stiffler

© 2020 Warner Press Inc.

Requests for information should be sent to:

Warner Press Inc.

P.O. Box 2499

Anderson, IN 46018

www.warnerpress.org

Kevin Stiffler • Editor

S. Katie Miller • Layout & Design

CONTENTS

The Warner Press *Relevance* Group Bible Studies provide intriguing examinations of topics using the whole of the Scriptures. The guides incorporate various stories and activities to introduce and apply the subject matter, with a Bible study component at the heart of each session. Our goal is to show life-long believers and those new to the faith how to know the Lord intimately while encouraging them to step out and join him in his work with miraculous results.

These flexible studies are ideal for any setting. We know that time is a valuable commodity in today's society, and that's why each book consists of five or six short lessons intended to meet the group's scheduling needs.

L1

Trouble between Brothers

Genesis 25:19–34; 27:1–29

Main Point

Trickery and selfish actions can cause damage and conflict in our relationships, as they did with Jacob and his brother Esau.

Background

Isaac and Rebekah's twin sons, Jacob and Esau, struggled with one another even in the womb. Isaac was partial to Esau, but Jacob was Rebekah's favorite. This encouraged rivalry between the sons. The impulsive Esau was willing to give up his inheritance to feed a craving, while Jacob displayed a readiness to use deceit to obtain a position that was not his own. Jacob's behavior had significant negative ramifications. God was at work in the midst of this family conflict to accomplish his plan to grow his people. But Jacob's selfishness and deceit disrupted the relationship between him and Esau.

Famous Siblings

Famous siblings—whether scriptural, fictional, or celebrity—often seem to capture our attention and dominate the headlines. Here are examples, some real and some fictional:

- Cain and Abel
- Joseph and his brothers
- Moses, Aaron, and Miriam
- Leah and Rachel
- The kids on *The Brady Bunch*
- Kyle and Kurt Busch (NASCAR)
- Maggie and Jake Gyllenhaal
- Karen and Richard Carpenter
- Jane and Peter Fonda
- The Marx Brothers
- John, Robert, and Edward Kennedy
- Jeb and George W. Bush

What seemed to characterize the relationships of some of these siblings? What grievances or sources of tension and conflict, if any, were present?

If you have any siblings, how would you characterize your own relationship with them? What factors have contributed to the relationship being as it is?

What do you consider to be the root causes of most sibling tensions or conflicts? What kind of effect do these tensions tend to have on the siblings and on the family as a whole?

What is different about the way Isaac approached the childlessness of his wife Rebekah versus the way his father Abraham approached the childlessness of his wife Sarah (see Gen 16)?

____

____

____

____

Because Esau was the favorite of his father and Jacob was the favorite of his mother, sides likely would have been taken and alliances formed on a number of issues. How can parents in any family take steps to prevent favoritism of children (real or perceived) from becoming a problem?

____

____

____

In the culture of that day, how might a love of hunting have been useful? How might a love of staying "at home among the tents" have been useful? How can different temperaments and interests among siblings make it more difficult for them to understand and empathize with each other?

____

____

II. Read Genesis 25:29–34.

Why would Esau give up his birthright for a simple bowl of stew? When have you seen someone forfeit a great blessing in a moment of weakness or foolishness? How can God provide restoration in these circumstances, and how do the parties involved still have to live with the consequences of their actions?

God had already indicated that the older sibling would serve the younger. Does this seem unfair to you? Explain. Tradition dictated that, as the eldest, Esau would inherit the property and assume the dominant role in the family. How might the closeness in the timing of the boys' deliveries have caused Jacob to feel about Esau's right to privilege and dominance?

What is the relationship between the gift of free will God gives us and the fact that God knew beforehand some aspects of the relationship between Jacob and Esau?

III. Read Genesis 27:1–29.

How might God's prophecy to Rebekah about her sons (Gen 25:23) have affected her behavior here? Was that any excuse? Explain. How do we balance the human dynamic of deception and conniving with the divine dynamic of what God has destined for certain people?

Do you think Isaac got "lazy" here? Should he have pressed more to make sure he was blessing Esau? Explain. What (if anything) might have been different if Isaac had learned the truth and saved his choicest blessing for the real Esau? How do the words we speak to and over our own children and the other children in our lives have power to affect these children?

____

____

____

____

Why would dastardly deeds such as those committed by Jacob and Rebekah be included in the biblical narrative?

____

____

____

What were the benefits promised to the descendants of Jacob/Israel by the blessing Isaac gave? How have these come to pass?

____

____

____

Reconciliation Needed

Peter's pastor encouraged congregation members to think about people in their lives with whom they needed reconciliation. Peter immediately thought of his only brother. They had not been on good terms for many years. Even since childhood, there seemed to be some obstacle between them that Peter could not clearly identify or understand.

For a while Peter had tried to work on the relationship, but when a letter arrived from his brother detailing Peter's shortcomings and faults, Peter gave up and stopped trying. Now he decided to take the high road. He would show kindness, love, and concern to his brother in every way possible.

Peter began to pray regularly for his brother. And soon another letter arrived, asking for forgiveness and reconciliation. After years of separation and anger, Peter and his brother had an opportunity for peace. They don't focus on the time they have missed; they treasure every opportunity for friendship.

To whom do you relate most closely in this story? Why?

How were the issues faced by Esau and Jacob similar to or different from family conflicts you are aware of today?

When have you experienced or seen the joy that comes through a mended relationship?

Tools for Reconciliation

Romans 12:18 states, "If it is possible, as far as it depends on you, live at peace with everyone." We cannot force others to live at peace with us if they choose not to do so. We can, however, forgive others in our hearts and live out of that forgiveness. We may still not be able to return to the relationship as it was before the conflict. But God can work through it all to help us mature and become more like Christ.

Think about how the following tools might help you find peace and reconciliation in the relationships in your life:

- Thanking God for the good things you have received or learned in a relationship, listing those gifts and recalling each situation.

- Praying Ephesians 3:16–19, inserting the name of the individual with whom you need to be reconciled in place of the word *you*.

- Making a conscious effort not to share with others about the wrong that has been done to you.

How have these principles been at work in your own personal experiences of reconciliation?

With whom would you like to experience reconciliation currently? Why?

How have you seen God bring about reconciliation in a church setting?

Justice or Mercy?

People tend to favor justice when others do wrong, and mercy when they themselves have done wrong. In our society, justice often seems to take a long time to be carried out. But there is a great concern that punishment not be inflicted on those who are not guilty of the crime they have been accused of.

God's way is often a blend of justice and mercy. Sometimes we can clearly see a connection between sinful choices and painful outcomes. At other times, it seems as though people get away with sin or are even blessed by God in spite of their unworthiness. We might object to this and find cause to question God—or we might see the redemptive hand of God making all things new and transforming failure into victory. We would do well to rejoice in the providence and plan of God.

If God were to always act according to your concept of justice, how much different would your life be? Why?

Deception led to great trouble in today's story from Genesis. What are some of the ways people today use deception? How might a better outcome be found with straightforward communication?

Closing Prayer

God, we seek your help and guidance for reconciliation in our relationships, regardless of how the problems started. Help us to understand the perspectives and experiences of others. We repent of words and deeds of deception that have caused conflict and pain. We bring to you areas of tension in our own families and ask that you show us how to take the first steps toward peace. Give us tools for reconciliation and hearts of love. Amen. ■

L2

The Reunion

Genesis 42:1–20; 43:1–15; 44:1–13; 45:1–15; 46:1–7

Main Point

The Old Testament story of Joseph and his brothers shows us the role of love, forgiveness, and God's hand in restoring broken relationships.

Background

Who could have seen the tragedies Joseph had suffered leading to good? At some point in time, Joseph began to see it that way. His brothers had considered killing him before deciding to sell him as a slave. Many years had passed, but Joseph never forgot about home, never forgot about his family. When the land of Canaan was racked by famine, Jacob sent his sons to Egypt to buy food. He (and they) never dreamed what they would find there. Much better than grain, they would be reunited with Joseph, who would forgive his brothers and secure their future.

Do What You Have to Do

The family farm in Oklahoma was struggling to produce much of a crop during the dust bowl of the 1930s. He took a chance and drove to California to seek a better life. One day after working in the fields there, he was standing outside his tent when she pulled in with her siblings and their parents, who had come from Arkansas seeking a better life. After he and she got married, they continued to live at the farm labor camp. He eventually built them a house with his own hands—hauling the lumber, running wire, and digging his own septic tank. After their first son was born, they scraped together enough money to move into town. The original house was still standing eighty years later, bearing testimony to the fact that sometimes you do what you have to do.

Think about a time you had to swallow your pride or do something you considered "beneath" you. What were the circumstances, and why did you respond as you did?

It has been said that we should *always* be kind to other people because we never know the private battles they are fighting. How have you found this to be true?

I. **Read** Genesis 42:1–20.

Do you think the loss of Joseph was still on Jacob's mind at this point? How about on the brothers' minds? Why do you say so?

What do you think was going through Joseph's mind when he saw his brothers? Do you think he really suspected them of being spies? Explain.

When painful memories from the past resurface and we are not able to address the situation in ways that resolve things, what are we to do? How can we find inner healing and move on toward a healthy future? What do we do when someone we have been in conflict with passes away before the situation can be resolved? Is it sometimes better to forget something bad from the past? Is it even possible to do? Explain.

II. Read Genesis 43:1–15.

Why do you think Joseph wanted his older brothers to bring back Benjamin, his younger brother? Genesis 35:16–20 provides one clue, but what other reasons might there have been?

Why do you think Joseph's brothers were honest with Joseph about the fact that they had a younger brother (Benjamin) still at home?

Why was Israel (Jacob) hesitant to send Benjamin down to Egypt? Although every child is unique and special, when have you seen favoritism cause problems in a family?

III. Read Genesis 44:1–13.

It almost seems as if Joseph was "having a little fun" with his brothers. Is this what was going on, or was it something else? Why do you say so? How did Joseph's actions indicate generosity and genuine concern but almost seem to demonstrate a hint of revenge at the same time?

IV. Read Genesis 45:1–15.

In what ways did God use Joseph to save the lives of his brothers? What was ironic about this situation? What did this "saving of lives" have to do with God's promise to Abraham, extended to Isaac and Jacob, that Abraham's descendants would become a great nation?

V. Read Genesis 46:1–7.

Why would God find it necessary to send Jacob and his family to Egypt in order to make a great nation out of them? Why not just accomplish that back home in Canaan?

What do you think had changed in Jacob over the years that he had ben apart from Joseph? What do you think had changed in Joseph during this time? What might have changed in Joseph's brothers? How could all of this have been used as a part of God's plan to save lives in the immediate context and down through the years to today?

Near or Far

Two brothers, now in their seventies, have been best friends all their lives. They live about thirty minutes from each other, but they still get together whenever they can—to eat lunch, to watch television, or for short camping trips. A man in his eighties who had six siblings called each of them every Sunday evening, back in the days of landlines and long-distance charges. For decades, three sisters met each week for coffee. Through divorces, sickness, and times of unimaginable heartache, these three women were faithful to get together for prayer, sharing, fellowship, and mutual encouragement.

If you have siblings, what is your relationship with them like now as compared to how it was in the past? If things have changed, why? What are some useful tools, approaches, and attitudes for honoring our siblings and expressing our love to them? (If you are an only child, you can answer these questions with respect to cousins, good friends, or others who are close to you.)

What is one way you would like to see your relationship with your siblings (or others close to you) change in the future? Why? What might make this change possible?

On the Mend

When a relationship with someone we love is broken, we try to cope with the pain, but it never seems to go away. We might manage to forget for a limited stretch of time, but our knowledge of the situation lies just beneath the surface, ready to bubble up at any moment. A holiday, a television show, a certain food, or even a particular smell can bring the memories rushing back again. We long for things to be mended, but life is so busy; we have our own families and jobs and lives to attend to. Maybe the person on the other end of the broken relationship has passed away and we never got a chance to make things right; this comes with its own set of challenges and difficulties. Of course, we can't force anyone to change, and we can't force anyone to love us.

Going forward, how might you approach your relationships with those you love in a more healthy fashion? "Ground rules" may be too formal of a term, but what sorts of basic things could you incorporate into your relationships to keep them healthy and growing, with open channels of communication and honesty from both parties?

Made for Relationships

Second Corinthians 5:17–20 says, "Therefore, if anyone is in Christ, the new creation has come: The old has gone, the new is here! All this is from God, who reconciled us to himself through Christ and gave us the ministry of reconciliation: that God was reconciling the world to himself in Christ, not counting people's sins against them. And he has committed to us the message of reconciliation. We are therefore Christ's ambassadors, as though God were making his appeal through us. We implore you on Christ's behalf: Be reconciled to God." Reconciliation with others is possible when we become new creations in Christ. This is not just a "cosmetic" makeover; it is a passing away of the old nature, the old way of doing things. God has named us as ambassadors of heaven; we are commissioned to be reconciled in our relationships and to let people know that the God of heaven loves them and wants to be in eternal fellowship with them—starting now.

What are the biggest barriers to healthy human relationships in today's society? What are the biggest barriers to healthy relationships between people and God? What can be done to break down these barriers?

Closing Prayer

God, we are inspired by Joseph's story because of the way he forgave and because of how you used the whole thing for good. We want to forgive as Joseph forgave, and we want to see you work in our lives and our relationships to reconcile others to you. We know that in Christ this is possible, so we pray that we will be sensitive and courageous as you teach us new ways of relating to others. Amen. ∎

The Neighbor

Luke 10:25–37

Main Point

The Parable of the Good Samaritan teaches us that a neighbor is anyone who shows mercy to us—and anyone who needs our mercy.

Background

The individual who asked the question that led to the Parable of the Good Samaritan was what we might call a learned theologian. But while the man's theoretical knowledge was necessary, it was also insufficient. One must proceed beyond reading or hearing to doing. Life under the rule and reign of God is active rather than theoretical. That Jesus made a despised Samaritan the hero of his story must have jarred the ears of his Jewish hearers. In the process Jesus included the Samaritan, and others like him, within the circle of the neighbors to whom mercy is to be extended.

Things That Divide

There are a number of barriers that divide people from one another. It is easy to spot physical barriers such as a fence around private property, a bodyguard at the side of a celebrity, or a cubicle designating someone's workspace in an office. But there are many barriers that are not always apparent to us or do not seem to be barriers at all. These things can cause division and misunderstanding and keep us from enjoying relationships to the full.

Think about how the barriers listed here separate you from others:

- Economic status
- Racial or ethnic identification
- Intellectual ability
- Faith tradition
- Lifestyle
- Language
- Gender
- Age

Which of these things make it difficult for you to reach out to other people, and why?

Which of these things are no problem for you, and why?

How have differences between you and other people (based on the barriers listed above or on other things) enriched your life?

I. Read Luke 10:25–29.

Though the text seems to indicate that the law expert may not have been particularly sincere when he asked the question "Who is my neighbor?" it is possible that the inquiry was not completely insincere. What do you think, and why? When is it right to "test" the advice someone gives us or to "test" whether a person who is giving us advice is worthy of our attention?

Jesus answered a question with a question, but he wasn't being rude or evasive; instead, he was helping the expert in the law to address a more important question. When have you asked a question and received an indirect response that helped you get at a deeper issue or an important truth?

When have you felt the need to justify yourself—your words, your actions, or a decision you made? What kinds of situations cause us to justify ourselves? Is this always wrong? Explain.

____

____

____

____

____

II. Read Luke 10:30–32.

In our own context, the rough equivalent of a priest might be a pastor, and the equivalent of a Levite might be another church staffer. What reasons might the priest or the Levite in this story have given for passing the wounded man by? What reasons do people give today for not helping the needy people they encounter? What criteria do you use when deciding whether to stop and help a stranded motorist, give money to someone outside a restaurant or store who is asking, or offer assistance in some similar situation? Why?

____

____

____

____

____

____

____

III. Read Luke 10:33–37.

Jesus made a hated individual, a Samaritan, the hero of this story. How do you think most Jews would have responded to this story of the Samarian's mercy? Why?

Does Jesus expect every one of his followers to drop everything every time they see someone in need in order to help? Explain.

We don't all have the money, the transportation, and the other resources needed to pick up injured travelers, care for their medical needs, and find them lodging. In what other ways can we be "neighborly" with the things God has given us?

Life under the rule and reign of God is concrete and active rather than abstract and theoretical. The law expert might have thought that he was having a purely theoretical discussion with Jesus about neighbors and the need to reach out to others. Jesus pointed him beyond theory to the need to put belief into practice. What is the relationship between knowledge and action when it comes to our faith?

Being a Neighbor

The world has billions and billions of people. Within that worldwide population there is impressive variety. There are racial variations, ethnic distinctions, and national peculiarities that are almost too numerous to count.

As Christians, we tend to glibly say that all people are God's children. Theoretically, we maintain that all men and women are our brothers and sisters. But things may play out much differently, in concrete reality, when a Methodist from Ohio meets a Muslim from Oman. We may not truly feel like brothers and sisters when we see people of other racial, ethnic, or economic backgrounds on the street. We may be hesitant to be the first to extend the hand of friendship or to respond if we see some of these people in trouble. We may not be very willing to take risks for them, as we would take risks for our family members and closest friends.

We say that God loves all people without partiality. And we say that our aim is to become more like Jesus, the Son who is the embodiment of the Father. So just what is our obligation to those who are different from us? Explain.

Effective Neighbors

Some churches have "benevolence policies" outlining how the congregation will assist those in need. Such policies may set aside a certain amount of funds to be given away and list the situations toward which those funds will be given (e.g., to assist with rent, to help with utility bills, etc.).

In one community, many churches partner together to help needy families. The individual congregations have their own food pantries, but those who wish to receive food must first call a central "clearinghouse" where a staff member confirms the people's identities, assesses their needs, and refers them to a specific church. This system helps to ensure that all churches can contribute and that the people who ask for food really need it.

From your own perspective, what are the most effective approaches and guidelines for churches to act as "neighbors" in helping others? Why?

Life Implications

Modern technology, conveniences, and lifestyles sometimes cause us to miss opportunities to connect with our neighbors. We work long days, drive home, pull into the garage, and press a button to shut the door. Our cell phones allow us to "screen" callers, ignoring those we don't feel like speaking with. And many of us do not answer a knock at the front door if we don't know who's there. Based on the Parable of the Good Samaritan, we might define a neighbor as "one who has mercy on others." This means that the people who live next door to us are not necessarily our neighbors, and that it is possible to be a neighbor to people who live nowhere near us.

What are the implications of the Parable of the Good Samaritan for your own life? How do you hope to live out the things you have learned? What changes will you need to make? Whom will you need to make a more concerted effort to reach out to in Christian love?

Closing Prayer

God, we know it is not always easy to break down barriers. Prejudices and entrenched perspectives can be difficult to change. But your Spirit has the power to change us. We ask you to generate love in the midst of hatred, trust in the midst of suspicion, mercy in the midst of malice, and compassion in the midst of indifference. Help us embrace the perspective and the love of Christ in all our relationships. Amen. ■

L4

The Ones Jesus Loved

John 11:1–44

Main Point

Jesus loved siblings Mary, Martha, and Lazarus, and he performed a miracle in which Lazarus, who had been dead for four days, was raised from the dead.

Background

The Sadducees rejected any belief in life after death, while the Pharisees taught that all the dead would be raised in a general resurrection at the end of time. Jesus was moved at the death of his friend Lazarus and the sorrow of those around him. He promised Martha that if she believed she would see God's glory. Perhaps Jesus had taught this family concerning the resurrection on some previous occasion. Or perhaps Lazarus and his sisters ascribed to the teaching of the Pharisees about eternal life. Whatever the case, Jesus' love for his friends was demonstrated, God's glory was revealed, and Lazarus was raised.

Death and Life

Are you a gardener? What do you know about growing things? Think about all of the tasks people do as a part of gardening. They prepare the dirt, plant seeds, water, fertilize, prune, pull weeds, compost, and eventually pick the harvest. Consider how many of these tasks carry an association with death. Dirt, fertilizer, and compost all have elements of things discarded, dead, or decaying. Seeds have to be planted—buried in the ground and consumed. Pruning is the cutting off and discarding of unproductive features. Even the process of harvesting involves separating fruit, vegetable, flower, or grain from its source of life.

Now, think how many of these functions carry an association with life. Answer: *all of them*. New plants and trees come from death. In order for new life to occur, something must die.

Imagine you were holding a whole, *overripe* apple. What might it be good for? What has to happen for us to have a "new crop" in life? How are fruit and seeds like death and resurrection?

I. **Read** John 11:1–16.

How do you think the sisters anticipated Jesus responding when they let him know about Lazarus? In what other ways might he have responded? What might have been the pros and cons of each?

Do you think every sick person was healed who came into contact with Jesus when he walked this earth? How about every sick person who came into contact with Peter or the other apostles after the Holy Spirit had come? Why or why not? What is the purpose of miraculous healing, and how (if at all) does its occurrence (or lack thereof) relate to its purpose? Explain.

II. Read John 11:17–37.

What did Martha seem to want from Jesus when he arrived?

What was it that moved Jesus in spirit and caused him to weep? Was it the death of his good friend Lazarus? the sorrow of Lazarus's sisters Mary and Martha, also good friends of the Lord? the inability of the disciples and Lazarus's family to better grasp the ability of Jesus to raise Lazarus from the dead? the specter of death and the pain it caused, which were not in God's original plan? Why do you say so?

Can you sympathize with how Mary and Martha must have felt? If so, why? If not, why not?

What sorts of emotions are represented in the tears of believers who weep when a fellow believer has died? How about in the tears of believers when a nonbeliever has died? How about the tears of a nonbeliever who has lost a loved one to death?

III. Read John 11:38–44.

What do you notice about the nature of Jesus' prayer here? What didn't it contain? What might be implied in it, and why? What was its purpose?

What sorts of emotions and reactions might have been stirred in the crowd in response to this miracle? Why?

How would you respond to the assertion that a believer today prayed for a dead person and this person was raised to life again in response? Why? Is this one of the "greater things" Jesus promised that those who believe in him would do (John 14:12)? Explain.

Even though Jesus miraculously raised Lazarus from the dead here, Lazarus went on to eventually die again at some point. Perhaps it was from old age or from sickness or an accident—we do not know. How do you think Lazarus's resurrection at this point impacted the rest of his life and the way he thought about death?

Close Relationships

Sometimes we can know someone so well, so intimately, that we seem to know that person's thoughts. We can finish his or her sentences.

Another characteristic of these close relationships is the fact that we can presume on these people in ways we could never do with others. My parents had friends such as this. Once, when we were evacuated from our house, we called them in the middle of the night to say we were on our way. My parents knew that we would be warmly received. They didn't have to ask if it was all right to come; they knew that already.

In some situations of life, it is dangerous to assume. But with relationships such as these, we *can* assume. Really, we are doing more than assuming. We know beyond the shadow of a doubt that the things we need will be freely given.

What did Martha reveal about her expectations when she met Jesus on the road?

____

____

Can you make any association between relationships such as these and the one Jesus had with the Father that led to the prayer he spoke at Lazarus's tomb? What kind of relationship do *you* have with the Father?

____

____

____

Loss Assessment

Think about some areas of your life where you have suffered loss and perhaps blamed God. In your mind, if God had answered your prayer, then you would still have what it is that you lost. Maybe you have suffered the loss of your health, the loss of a loved one, the loss of a marriage or relationship, or something else.

List here some of the losses you have experienced:

Now pick one of the things from the list that you really regret losing. How can you claim a resurrection for this thing? Do you believe God can bring life out of the loss? If so, how? Remember, in the new life things may look somewhat different from how they did before. What might be your part in bringing this new life to pass?

We tend to be pretty good at holding onto belief in the resurrection of the body. We anticipate it with great joy and hope. But how can Jesus also help us to "live while living"? How can he bring resurrection power and new life to our relationships and to the circumstances we encounter each day?

Closing Prayer

God, thank you for the story of Mary and Martha and Lazarus. Thank you for the love you had for your friends and for the love you have for us and for calling us friends as well. Thank you for the many ways you bring new life, including in our relationships. Help us to venture forth today in belief and act in obedience as you direct, so that we may experience your glory and new life in our relationships. Amen. ∎

L 5

Still Friends

John 21

Main Point

After a night of fishing, the disciples joined the resurrected Jesus in fellowship, and Jesus then affirmed Peter by asking him to care for Jesus' sheep.

Background

Simon Peter and some of the other disciples were uncertain what the future held, so they turned back to what they used to know—fishing. When Jesus called out some advice to them and they followed it, they found a net-full of abundance. When they went back to shore and sat with Jesus for a meal, they were even more fully convinced that Jesus was really alive. Peter had denied knowing Jesus on the Lord's path to suffering, but Jesus invited him back into partnership and ministry. Jesus wanted Peter to put away the mistakes of the past, not compare himself to others, and surrender his future to the Lord.

Sharing a Meal

There are great benefits to sitting down and sharing a meal as a family. When family members spend time around the table together eating and conversing, they become physically healthier, less prone to disease and obesity, and stronger emotionally. Enjoying food together is a bonding experience that provides people with the opportunity to share their thoughts, feelings, and burdens with one another and offer mutual support.

Today, fewer families spend mealtimes together because of conflicting schedules. Families also have more distractions, primarily in the area of technology. Some families have recognized this and have attempted to limit distractions so they can build stronger relationships and share positive experiences around the table.

During the Last Supper, Jesus shared with his disciples around the table. At the table, Jesus taught them about service, sacrifice, and forgiveness. At the table, he provided for their physical needs and also encouraged their hearts.

What do you enjoy about experiences around the table with family and friends? How often do you share a meal with those you love?

What meals do you recall where you experienced the presence of the Lord with you in a special way? Describe these situations.

I. Read John 21:1–6.

Why do you think Peter and the other disciples headed back to fishing? Do you think their lack of success was caused by God as a "set-up" for their encounter with Jesus, or was it just due to natural circumstances? Explain.

People have long debated whether there is some significance to the fact that exactly 153 fish were caught. Some have speculated that the 153 fish represented all the species of fish known to be in existence at the time. Others find a match with the 153 people Jesus personally blessed in all of the Gospel accounts. What do you think, and why?

Why do you think the disciples did not recognize Jesus at first? Has there ever been a time when you did not recognize God at work in your life? Explain.

II. Read John 21:7–14.

What was the response of the disciples to the miracle they witnessed? Have you ever experienced a miracle in your life? If so, describe it. What were the results of that miracle?

How could the disciples have been uncertain whether it was Jesus? Was it the initial distance from the boat to the shore, the fact that they did not yet believe he was alive again, the fact that his appearance was somehow different, some combination of factors, or something else entirely? Explain.

III. Read John 21:15–17.

Why do you think Jesus asked Peter three times if he loved him? What might be the link to Peter's earlier denial of Jesus (John 18:15–18, 25–27)?

Have you ever felt pain in your heart when the Lord revealed truth that went right to the core of who you are, such as when Jesus questioned Peter? If so, how did you deal with the situation?

How can the hurts of the past keep us from moving forward in loving Jesus and serving and following him?

IV. Read John 21:18–25.

Have you ever compared your spiritual journey to the journeys of others? What happens when we do this?

What "other things" do you suppose Jesus did that are not listed in the Book of John or any of the other Gospels? How are the things we do know about Jesus sufficient for us to place faith in him as the Son of God, the sacrifice for our sins, and the giver of eternal life?

Who or what is the true source of contentment in this life? Explain.

What progress have you seen in your relationships with others and with your spiritual growth when you have kept your focus on Jesus?

Losing Focus

Jesus' disciples were not certain what they should do. They were no longer following in his footsteps, experiencing his daily ministry with him. Without direction, they returned to what they used to know and what they used to do. However, they were not successful. They worked hard, but their labors were fruitless. It was not until they encountered Jesus that their efforts had meaning. They experienced abundance and success when they followed his directions.

Have you ever been in a situation where you lost your focus or did not know what God wanted you to do next? If so, describe the experience. How did you respond?

Have you ever had an experience where you tried to do things on your own—in your own way and in your own timing, instead of following God's leading? What happened?

Have you ever had an experience where God directed you take a certain step and you obeyed? What happened in that situation?

How does it feel to know that God can use us in spite of our failures or shortcomings? How can we keep our focus on Christ and what he is calling us to do?

Past and Future

Peter had made mistakes in the past, and he certainly felt the weight of that. Jesus demonstrated love for Peter as he called Peter into his service, despite Peter's previous failures. Peter experienced healing from his past and received his mission for the future. He knew that choosing this path would result in suffering, but he was committed to following Jesus. The early church was inspired and grew because of Peter's leadership.

Do you feel discouraged by something in your past, believing that it will keep you from following God or that it will keep God from using your life to make an impact? If so, describe the situation. How does today's passage encourage you in this area?

Have you ever compared yourself to another person and felt discouraged about yourself in regard to your spiritual growth or your relationship with God? Explain. How does today's passage encourage you in this area?

Have you ever feared following Jesus because of what it may cost you? If so, explain. What can we learn from Peter and the other disciples about following the Lord?

How has God used your life as a blessing or encouragement to others?

The Cost of Commitment

In Jesus' relationship with Peter, Jesus called Peter to commitment. Peter faced the choice of whether or not to follow Christ, and he made the decision to follow—even though it would eventually cost him his life. He was aware of the challenges, but decided that committing to follow the Lord was worth it. He put aside his fears and failures, learned not to compare himself to others, and picked up his cross. We face a similar decision today. Jesus is aware of our past mistakes, but he invites us to journey with him to fish for people and care for our brothers and sisters in the body of Christ.

Will you follow Jesus? Will you trust him with all that you are, with all that you have? Will you give him complete control over your body, your mind, and your heart? There is a cost involved and the decision is not easy, but in Christ you can find forgiveness, love, acceptance, and purpose. What is your decision today? Express your commitment in the space provided.

Closing Prayer

God, we know that our actions and attitudes have sometimes been inconsistent with the faith we profess. Today we ask you to provide direction and purpose for our lives—the "miraculous catch" we need. We believe that you have a call and commission for each of us. We ask you to give us discernment and boldness as we step up, move forward, and press in to your perfect will. We eagerly anticipate your response. Amen. ∎

L 6

Don't Play Favorites

James 2:1–13

Main Point

The Book of James teaches that Christians should make no distinctions in their relationships based on the economic or social status of others.

Background

Today's study has to do with how we treat and value other people. It warns against favoring the wealthy over the poor, which can amount to a put-down of the poor—and overrating the rich and famous. James tells us that this kind of treatment is sinful and can be remedied by following the royal law in our relationships. The royal law simply put is this: "Love your neighbor as yourself" (James 2:8). James further elaborates on what that really means by suggesting that we approach our relationships with the poor—and with everyone else, for that matter—with respect, mercy, and loving kindness.

Think of a time when you were rejected. Write down some words that express how you felt.

In what situations or relationships would it particularly bother you to be "out of favor"? In what cases would it hardly bother you at all? Why the difference?

I. Read James 2:1–4.

In the larger context, the Book of James was originally written to believers who were undergoing persecution for their faith. While its words are certainly applicable even to believers who are not being persecuted, how does this context change your understanding of what James was saying here?

Whether or not it's as deliberate as suggested in the text, how do those in our society today seem to show favoritism toward some people and discriminate against others? Does eliminating favoritism and discrimination mean that everyone will have the same "stuff"—money, kind of house, possessions, etc.? As a society, how can we help to ensure that all people have the same opportunities without restricting the rights and freedoms of anyone?

Prior to Jesus coming, many people thought that health, wealth, and many children were direct signs of God's favor, while sickness, poverty, and no children were signs that God disapproved of you or that you had sinned. How might such an understanding cause favoritism and discrimination?

II. Read James 2:5–11.

Why would someone who had little material wealth be more open to God's kingdom?

In what ways should James's assertion that God has "chosen those who are poor in the eyes of the world to be rich in faith and to inherit the kingdom he promised those who love him" (v 5) be encouraging to us? In what ways should this be challenging to us?

In what ways do the wealth and power of the rich enable them to exploit, take advantage of, and otherwise "dishonor" those who are poor? How is this seen in the courtroom or in situations having to do with the enforcement and the breaking of laws?

Why is "loving your neighbor as yourself" an area in which it is particularly easy to break God's law?

According to the standard James gave here, we have all broken God's laws. Is it possible to love our neighbors and still show favoritism, commit adultery, or commit murder? Explain.

III. Read James 2:12–13.

If God's law tells us some things not to do—including not showing favoritism—then how is it a "law that gives freedom" (v 12)? What kind of freedom is this referring to, and what's so good about it?

How does the saying "What goes around, comes around" apply to these verses?

When it comes to God's treatment of us, why is it important that "mercy triumphs over judgment"? Why is this important in our treatment of other people?

Living the Royal Law

Today's Bible passage defines the "royal law" as "Love your neighbor as yourself," originally found in Leviticus 19:18. Interestingly, the verse in Leviticus is part of a list subtitled in some Bible versions, "Various Laws." These laws addressed a wide range of areas, including treatment of one's parents, offering sacrifices, picking crops, paying workers, treatment of those with disabilities, and the use of weights and measurements in business.

Why might the people in the Old Testament, the people James originally wrote to, and followers of Christ today need a reminder such as "Love your neighbor as yourself"?

Based on your understanding of the "royal law," finish the following statement. In your response, consider concepts such as showing kindness, showing mercy, extending forgiveness, showing respect to everyone, looking beyond the exterior, trying to put yourself in the other person's shoes, praying for those who are unlike you, trying to see each person through God's eyes, and treating others as you would like to be treated: *I commit myself to living the royal law, and loving others impartially with the love of Christ, by…*

Favoritism and Discrimination

Visiting a new church can be intimidating. Perhaps you are still in the same church you grew up in or have been a part of for many years. Maybe you have switched churches, but you already knew a lot of people at your new church and had visited there before, so you already had personal connections and knew what to expect.

Try to think about it from the perspective of a newcomer. *Will anyone talk to me? Will I know the songs that are sung during worship? Will this church expect me to give money today? Will I be put on the spot because I am new?* It's true that we should be mature enough to offer grace to others who are trying to welcome us in. But favoritism and discrimination can be subtle; they can silently creep into our attitudes and behaviors so that we are scarcely aware of their presence.

What instances of favoritism have you seen in the church? What situations have you seen in which someone was being judged by outward appearances? Where have you seen prejudice and discrimination practiced? Where have you seen people being treated unfairly or disrespectfully? What can you do about it?

A Loving Life

The "royal law" from Leviticus 19:18 was used by Jesus in his own teaching. When he was asked to identify the greatest commandment, he responded that we should love God with our entire being and "Love your neighbor as yourself" (Matt 22:34–40). Love itself is a gift of God. We must open that gift and use it. God will help us with his wisdom as we deal with thorny issues and questions related to loving others; we just need to ask. This doesn't mean loving others will always be easy, but the Holy Spirit can guide us into actions and reactions that build relationships rather than destroy them, that affirm people rather than devalue them. We need to see people as persons to be treasured rather than as individuals who can stoke our egos as we position ourselves in the glow of their prestige or as they help us get ahead. Rather than welcoming those we think can benefit us and shunning those who seem of no use to us, we must embrace all with the love of Christ.

How can you keep loving others and living a life that is clearly shaped and guided by that love?

Closing Prayer

God, we know how easy it is to judge others. We know how easy it is to look at people or hear them talk and make the immediate judgment, "I know where they are coming from." Help us to see with your eyes and to listen with your ears. May our relationships be full of your love and kindness. May we find the courage to act with respect. We truly want to be your disciples of love and caring. Amen. ∎

Notes